Original French edition:
François le pauvre d'Assise
© 2009 by Fleurus-Mame, Paris
© 2011 by Ignatius Press, San Francisco • Magnificat USA LLC, New York
All rights reserved
ISBN Ignatius Press 978-1-58617-623-5
ISBN Magnificat 978-1-936260-18-8

Printed by Tien Wah Press, Malaysia
Printed on June 15, 2011
Job Number MGN 11007
Printed in Malaysia in compliance with the Consumer Protection Safety Act, 2008.

Francis
The Poor Man of Assisi

Text: Juliette Levivier – Illustrations: Claire de Gastold

Translated by Janet Chevrier

Ignatius

MAGNIFICAT®

How beautiful Assisi was in that lovely spring of 1182! The city seemed to slumber under the warm Italian sun!

The sight of the pretty little town perched on a hill filled Pietro Bernardone with contentment. He was almost back home after weeks away selling his fabrics in France. But, who was this running down the road toward him at full tilt?

It was Masseo, his neighbor's little son.

3

"Mister Pietro, Mister Pietro, come quickly! While you were away, your wife, Dona Pica, gave birth to your baby!"

Pietro Bernardone's heart skipped a beat! His baby was born!

"It's a fine little boy!" said the child. "His name is Giovanni. Come quickly!"

Pietro Bernardone started running up the rocky road. What a steep climb, but he did not even notice!

He could not wait to see his son and hug his wife.

"I think, Masseo, that we're going to change my little boy's name. If Dona Pica agrees, I'd like to call him Francis."

"Francis? But, who's ever heard of a name like that?"

"Francis means 'the Frenchman'. He was born while I was away in France, and Dona Pica is French, you know! It would be a nice mark of respect for her and for France, which is such a lovely country."

At last they arrived. How happy he was! Pietro hurried into the house, bursting with joy.

6

$\mathcal{F}$rancis grew up. He liked enjoying himself and going out with his friends. His father was a hard worker. He was well known and respected by all. But Francis sometimes found him a bit too strict.

"Work, work, work," Francis grumbled, "that's all fine. But life is short! A boy needs to have fun, too!"

$\mathcal{F}$rancis was merry and generous. He was so amusing and so charming that everyone was glad to forgive him all his pranks, except maybe when he tore through the streets making a lot of noise in the middle of the night!

"Look, it's Francis! He's dressed up like a troubadour, and he's juggling tomatoes!"

What a happy-go-lucky fellow, that Francis!

Francis was twenty years old when war broke out between Assisi and the neighboring town of Perugia. He did not hesitate a second: he took up arms to defend his beloved city. He had always dreamed of becoming a knight!

"You'll see", he told his friends, "what a victory we will have!"

Alas! Assisi lost, and Francis was taken prisoner. He spent a whole year in a gloomy prison in Perugia. When he at last returned home, he was exhausted and ill.

This terrible ordeal left its mark on Francis.

Dona Pica was worried. "He's not our Francis! He used to be so full of life. But he never plays pranks or tells jokes anymore."

"Don't worry so much", said Pietro Bernardone to his wife. "He's just settled down a little. And that's all for the good, don't you think?"

But not long afterward, Francis recovered and was once again dreaming of glory. He enlisted in the Pope's army and prepared to go back to war. He would at last become a knight—it was now or never!

The Poor Man of Assisi

And so Francis left to join the Pope's army, then at war against the Roman emperor. But along the way, he fell ill and had to stop in the town of Spoleto.

He was lying in bed when suddenly a voice spoke to him, "Where are you going?"

"To Apulia, to become a knight in the service of the Pope", answered Francis with surprise. "What do you wish me to do, Lord?"

"Tell me, Francis, who do you think can better reward you, the Master or the servant?"

"The Master!"

"Why, then, do you seek to follow the servant instead of the Master? Go home . . . There you will learn what you must do."

This was the voice of Jesus! His instructions were clear. Deeply troubled, Francis obeyed and went home to Assisi.

Something had changed inside him. From then on, it was God who came first in his heart. It was God he wished to serve and to love.

Francis stopped going out to have fun with his friends. He preferred the company of the poor and the sick.

One morning while he was out riding his horse, Francis met a leper.* He trembled with fear. Ever since he was little, he had been so afraid of lepers that he refused to go near them. But Francis had truly changed. Overcoming his disgust, he got off his horse, went to the poor man, and kissed his hand. God knows how hard that was for him to do! But he who had once run away from lepers now reached out to them. The love of Jesus in his heart was stronger than anything!

From that day on, Francis often went to visit and help the lepers of Assisi.

*A person sick with leprosy, a highly contagious, disfiguring disease, common at the time

Francis moved into a mossy little grotto—a cave—near Assisi. It was not very comfortable, but what did he care! Surrounded by nature, which he dearly loved, Francis was completely content. He gave thanks to the Lord with all his heart!

One day, as he was praying in the chapel of San Damiano, Francis heard the voice of Jesus once again.

It was coming from the big crucifix hanging above the altar: "Go, Francis, and repair my house, which has fallen into ruin."

And, indeed, the little chapel was in a sorry state! But where could he find the money to repair it? Francis took his father's most beautiful fabrics and sold them. With the money he made, he bought building stones and roof tiles and began the repairs with his own two hands.

When Pietro Bernardone found out, he was furious. He dragged his son before Guido, the bishop of the town, to demand justice.

But . . . what happened then? Francis began undressing in front of everyone! He handed his clothing back to his father, saying to him: "Here! Until today, I have called you my father. But from now on, the only one I shall call Father is Our Father who art in heaven. He is all my wealth, and I place all my faith in him."

Deeply moved, Bishop Guido covered Francis with his cloak.

From that moment on, the Church would be his true home.

*F*rancis returned to work with enthusiasm. People brought him building materials and came to help him. He lived in the greatest simplicity.

"My friend is Lady Poverty!" he said.

But, little by little, Francis sensed through prayer that Jesus wanted something more of him.

*O*ne day, as he was listening to a priest reading the Gospel, he suddenly understood what the Lord expected of him: his mission was to proclaim the Gospel along the roads. Like the disciples of Jesus, he would go in poverty, without sandals, without a walking stick.

$\mathcal{A}$nd so it was that he set out on the roads, barefoot and dressed in an odd tunic made of very rough cloth. Francis' overflowing love of Jesus touched the many people who came to listen to him.

$\mathcal{O}$ne morning, Francis saw two of his friends arriving.

"Bernardo, Pietro, how happy I am to see you!"

"Francis, we, too, want to give our lives to Christ."

18

Francis' joy was immense. How happy the new brothers were! Soon, other young men came to join them. They formed a little community that Francis called the Friars Minor, which means the littlest brothers of Jesus. They lived in great poverty, praying fervently. Going off two by two, they spoke to the crowds, who listened to them eagerly. The number of brothers grew and grew. That is when Francis decided to write a rule, in order to organize their way of life. But, for that, he needed the Pope's approval . . .

Francis set off for Rome to present the community of Friars Minor to Pope Innocent III. Just before his arrival, the Pope had had a very strange dream: the earth had shaken, the great Basilica of Saint John Lateran, in the heart of Rome, had begun to crack. It was about to collapse when, all of a sudden, a little man had appeared, dressed in a rough brown tunic. He had pushed the walls back up and had held up the roof. The earth had stopped quaking.

Phew, the church had been saved!

That little man, the Pope recognized him as soon as he met him: it was Francis, the poor man of Assisi!

Innocent III understood that Francis and his brothers had a great mission to fulfill. The Pope told him about his dream. And suddenly Francis grasped the meaning of Jesus' words: it was not the little church of San Damiano that he had to rebuild—it was the great Church of Jesus!

Back in Assisi, Francis went to preach in one of the churches. Clare, a young woman who lived nearby, listened to him with all her heart. She was overwhelmed by what she heard! For a long time, she had wanted to give her life to God and felt him calling her to live with "Lady Poverty". She decided to join Francis, who welcomed her with joy. Bishop Guido gave his approval to Clare's plan and allowed her to go live near the San Damiano chapel. Other young women came to join her.

They founded the Order of Poor Ladies.

Clare and Francis remained great friends all their lives. They loved to meet for long talks about Jesus.

Brother Francis

Francis loved nature. He liked to go for walks in the country with Brother Leo. Francis so admired his simplicity of heart and soul. During these walks, Francis would speak to birds, which gathered gently around him to listen.

"Praise God, Brother Birds. He takes care of you without your having to do a thing!"

Then, turning to his friend, he added: "Look, Brother Leo, just look how beautiful these birds are! And our Brother Sun, and our Sisters the Moon and the Stars, how wonderful it all is! I would like to sing forever the glory of God—and for all God's creatures to sing along with me!"

One day as he was passing through the village of Gubbio, Francis heard that a huge wolf was terrorizing the whole region. He made a big sign of the cross before setting off in search of the wolf. And there he was, coming toward him with his big jaws wide open, ready to devour Francis.

"Come here, Brother Wolf", Francis said calmly.

And, with that, as gentle as a lamb, the wolf came to lie at Francis' feet!

"On behalf of Christ, I command you to do no harm, to me or anyone else. You have done terrible misdeeds, wounding and killing God's creatures. But, if you are nice, Brother Wolf, the people here will forgive you and will give you food to eat. That way, you will never be hungry anymore, and you will no longer have to go about devouring people and animals."

It was a deal! The wolf placed his paw in Francis' hand. Never again would he hurt anyone. It is even said that it was he who watched over the children of the village when their parents were away!

The Friars Minor continued to grow in numbers. They traveled far and wide, preaching the word of the Gospel. Francis, too, traveled a great deal. In the company of a few brothers, he even journeyed to the Holy Land, where Jesus had lived. The trip was long, and Francis arrived very tired. But he had not lost any of his enthusiasm: he wanted all men to know and love Jesus.

Francis met the sultan of Egypt, who became his friend. With the sultan's permission, he had the overwhelming joy to visit Jerusalem and to pray on the hill of Golgotha where Jesus had died.

rancis went home to Italy. When he was not traveling the roads proclaiming the Gospel, he liked to retreat to the mountains on his own. He would stay in a grotto or a simple hut made of branches and spend all his time in prayer. He was happy to be able to devote himself to God and God alone.

It would soon be Christmas, Francis' favorite feast. He decided to celebrate the birth of Jesus in a very special way in the village of Greccio.

"I need a donkey and an ox, Brother Leo, and nice little sheep and plenty of hay!"

"But what for, Francis?"

"I want to recreate a grotto like the one in which our Savior was born. If the Pope allows it, we'll celebrate the Nativity there, with all the villagers of Greccio."

"What a good idea!"

The Pope gave his permission, and the villagers celebrated the birth of Jesus in a stable in the middle of the night—and this was the first living Nativity scene ever.

But Francis grew more and more tired. He was often ill and felt he would die soon. He set off with his faithful friend Leo for the mountains, where he so loved to withdraw to pray.

One morning, while he was praying before the grotto in which he had been living, a magnificent angel appeared to him. It had six wings and was flying gently toward Francis. All at once, its face changed: it was the face of Jesus! Filled with love, Francis suddenly felt a terrible pain. His hands, feet, and side were marked by the same five wounds that Jesus had suffered on the Cross! Francis had always tried to imitate Jesus, and now Jesus had allowed him to share in his suffering and his Passion.

Francis died two years later, with his heart fixed on Jesus whom he so loved.

Feast Day

Saint Francis' feast day is October 4. He is the patron saint of wolf cubs (thanks to the wolf of Gubbio!).

The Poverello of Assisi

Saint Francis was called the "Poverello", which means "poor little man" in Italian.

The Friars Minor, or Franciscans

In 1208, Bernardo da Quintavalle and Pietro Cattani joined Francis to share his life of prayer and preaching.
They were very quickly joined by other young men. As early as 1210, Pope Innocent III gave his approval
to this new community. Francis chose the name of Friars Minor in reference to the "little ones"
often spoken of in the Gospels. Today, they are also called Franciscans.
There are about 17,600 Franciscans spread throughout the world.

Clare of Assisi wanted to put into practice the same ideals as Francis. She joined him in 1212.
Together they founded a second order exclusively for women, the Order of Poor Ladies. Today they are known
as the Poor Clares or Clarisse. There are currently about 17,000 Poor Clares in 700 monasteries.

In 1221, Francis founded a third order reserved for those who, without becoming a religious,
wish to lead a spiritual life following the example of Saint Francis.
This is called the Secular Franciscan Order. About 400,000 members live in 30 countries.

The Franciscan Order has given birth to many other religious orders: Cordeliers (now known as Conventuals),
Celestines, Capuchins, Annonciades, etc. The Franciscan family is very big and as active as ever!

The Franciscan Habit

Franciscans wear a dark brown or gray-black habit with a round hood, a rope belt, and leather sandals.

The Little Flowers (or Fioretti) of Saint Francis

These little anecdotes, some true, some fictional, relate episodes from the life of Saint Francis,
such as the one about the wolf of Gubbio. They have been passed down by popular tradition.
Whether amusing or moving, they all show the saint's deep intimacy with Jesus.